Vipassana Meditation

A descent into the depths of the soul

Adrian Benea

Prologue

In the autumn of 2019 I passed through the gates of Vipassana retreat center, left my stuff in the lobby's locker and went to my designated room.

Ten days later, the one who left was a different person.

Different in what way? How is it possible that ten days of silent retreat can permanently alter a person's perspective on life?

The short version is that in those ten days I discovered how my personal hell looked like, how I built it by myself, and how absolutely and definitely painful it was. I learned that all aggressive, dismissive gestures, hurtful words I ever posed had consequences. That I don't get away with anything. Sooner or later every hurtful gesture I ever posed will invariably come back haunting me. I learned that karma is as real as it can be, but it's an internal event, not an external one.

The long version constitutes the subject of this book.

The reason I write it is to document a life changing experience that could prove useful to those who lived similar experiences but didn't completely made sense of them, or to those who wish to partake in a similar spiritual adventure but would like to have a sneak peek into it before deciding if it's worth it for them.

It could prove useful to those who are living a spiritual crisis, who feel something vital is missing from their lives. For all those who are looking for an alternative to the modern life.

It could prove useful to know we don't really need a religion to fill the God shaped form in our souls.

So let's dive in.

Interlude

It was towards the end of an exquisite summer, and I noticed again that peculiar gloomy feeling which in my case invariably coincides with the first leaves tumbling to the soil. I had short and long term plans, as usual, but they were quite vague, unsatisfactory, none of them really captivated me. I felt quite lost. I didn't have a strong sense of meaning in my life, never had. It is common knowledge, I suppose, that since we gave up religion, we don't know how to live our lives anymore. The religious man has a purpose in his life. Most of us, modern people, on the other hand, we live with the idea that we can invent our own meaning. From the ashes of religions, ideologies were born, and we all know how that played out, mass graves are there to prove it. As well as new philosophy schools, like existentialism, which didn't help fix the problem, yet it allowed us to conceptualize and to clarify it.

I began to understand — or maybe "understand" is an overstatement — I have started feeling that without a spiritual discipline we are doomed. We don't control ourselves; we are clearly unable to control ourselves enough to be able to motivate ourselves optimally. Our motivations are weak, circumstantial. Think of all those times when you decided you would pick up a sport or join a gym. You even paid for pretty expensive gears and a gym membership. How long did it take until you gave up?
We require an external force to thrust us intently in a specific direction. We can't create and sustain that force. It's almost impossible. There are some exceptions here and there, of course, but for the most of us this scenario is out of reach.

And I remembered then that I had for a long time wanted to experience this silent meditation retreat, to see what will happen if I dive deep enough into my mind, if I explore my soul. It was genuine curiosity, with a hint of hope, hope that I'll come out with some deep insights from the belly of the beast.

About three years ago I watched a documentary, "Doing time, doing Vipassana" about the largest prison in New Delhi, where someone suggested to organize a Vipassana meditation session as a means of social integration of the soon to be ex-detainees.
They did it and the outcome was outstanding.
The documentary follows the story of prison inmates who underwent profound changes. They came to realize that incarceration was not a dead end but the dawn of an improved, morally superior kind of life.

I witnessed the detainees claiming that Vipassana meditation completely changed their lives, they understood things they had never fathomed until that point.

Of course, we can speculate that they were conditioned to respond in this particular way; the documentary could have been scripted. Honestly, I don't think so and here is the reason why: I noticed their gestures, facial expressions, non-verbal clues, and they came across as genuine. It seemed to me that what those people were saying was as authentic as possible.

Since I saw that documentary, an idea persisted somewhere in the back of my mind: the idea that there is an experience out there that can totally change people's lives and do so in a surprisingly brief period of time.

An experience accessible to (almost) anyone, who requires only ten days of your life. And it's free, Vipassana centers operate on a donation basis. They survive off the donations of those who have gone through these retreats, and the mere fact that they are capable to function from only those contributions is probably the best argument for the effectiveness of the program.

Because under no circumstances would people pay substantial sums of money for something that would bring them a minor or no benefit at all. I don't see why they would do that.

At one point, at a party, I meet a couple, husband and wife, who had undertaken this retreat together. They seemed vaguely confused when they recounted the experience. I felt that... In fact no, I can't say I felt they didn't grasp what happened to them, maybe they just didn't know how to express all of that, maybe it was something ineffable for them. And I can understand that, I understand because I equally found it difficult to explain my experience in a concrete, concise way, for everyone to grasp. It's one of those experiences which you need to personally live to be able to properly understand.

I had this idea in mind for about three years. In the meantime, I had read more on the subject. I even made timid attempts to enroll in the Quebec's Vipassana Center, because it was the handiest, as I live in Montreal. I found out, to my surprise, that the open places were vanishing really quickly. Every time I tried to register, the seats were already occupied. Even the waiting list was always full.

Therefore, I said to myself: "look, you have a three-weeks vacation. You can choose your time and place. It doesn't have to be in Quebec; it can be somewhere else, in Asia for example. It is easier to find a place there."

And I started looking for Vipassana centers all over the world. I was attracted by the idea of doing the retreat in Asia primarily because of the weather. I know it's rainy season this time of year, but it's warm anyways. And the rain doesn't affect me, as I would pass my time inside, meditating.

During this period, in Canada and in the northern part of the United States, it starts to get cold, especially in the mountain areas. And I didn't know what the accommodation conditions would be. I didn't want to find myself freezing in a tent.

By chance, I ended up doing my retreat at the Dhamma Dhara Center, West of Boston. The period matched perfectly with my vacation and the waiting list was still open. I signed up and waited, fingers crossed, to receive the acceptance message. I didn't have high hopes, but I suspected that the staff would check all the files and eliminate those who could potentially have a hard time to cope with the ten intense days.

They insist on the fact that the retreat is not recommended to those who are depressed or have some kind of mental troubles, even mild ones. I didn't understand why this insistence, but it became clear as light soon after the retreat begun.

About two weeks later, I received an answer: I was accepted. I felt happy, excited, but also slightly anxious.

The Dhamma Dhara Center is about 400 km from Montreal. A short road trip was waiting for me, a kind of trip which was invariably a pleasure. I enjoyed being alone with my thoughts, or listen to music, audio books, podcasts.

I googled up the place for comprehensive information and, to my pleasant surprise, I found out that it is the first Vipassana center in North America. I had a good feeling about that, because about two years before I have enrolled in a yoga retreat at the Sivananda Center in Quebec and I was surprised to learn the same thing, that it was the first Sivananda Center in North America. There's no need to say I enjoyed every second of that retreat, and I hoped to repeat the same great experience this time also.

It seems obvious to me that if they are the first ones, if they survived so many years and developed to such an extent, it's because what these centers achieve is so overwhelmingly positive that people support them without hesitation.

The arrival

The weather is cold at the end of September in the mountain area where Vipassana Center is located. Because I didn't know what to expect, I was prepared for everything: warm clothing, a thick blanket, sleeping bag, pillow.

I woke up early in the morning. I'm not the only one, my neighbours are preparing for their work day, I can almost hear the sound of coffee pouring into the mugs and the soft, quiet morning yawning of those who drink it. I stop by a coffee shop to get one of those caramel macchiato that I love so much, although I do my best not to overindulge in. My metabolism is slower at my age, and even if I do my best to keep in shape by doing yoga and lifting weights, I cannot out train a bad diet. But today it's a special day, I allow myself to make an exception.

The trip didn't start well. At the Canadian-American border I had the mischance to be randomly selected for an "in detail" search. Actually I'm not that sure it was random, they asked about my destination and I told them about the retreat. It could be that border agents are trained to associate spiritual activities with drug use. That could explain the drug sniffing dog who enthusiastically spun around my car.

And I don't blame them, this is the unfortunate reality: Some of the modern spirituality seekers choose to reach their destination through drug induced revelations.

I'm not sure it's a good idea. "Beware of unearned wisdom," Carl Gustav Jung used to say, and it seems to me that there are obvious reasons for this.

I waited in the custom border building lobby, watching through the windows two border agents taking apart my car, searching through my stuff in the trunk.

The oversized windows should allow a lot of light through, yet the dirt on the panes leaves it dull to the point of depression. "Isn't this such a perfect allegory for life?," I thought to myself.

I observed them while sipping my coffee and I felt a slight uneasiness. Not because I had something to conceal, but because the doubts about the decision of joining the retreat crept out again.

We are creatures of habit and comfort and anything that gets us out of our comfort zone makes us anxious.

I had hidden my doubts from my friends, and no one seemed to be surprised by my decision, they are used to my self-discovery journeys.

This time though, I wasn't even near as confident in my choice. It was a silent retreat. We were not supposed to talk or make eye contact with our fellow colleagues.

Can you imagine what it means for a person who lives in the internet era not to talk, read, or make eye contact for ten days? What it means to remove any kind of distractions? No phone, no internet, no magazines or books, not even an agenda to write down your thoughts?

In prison they call it "solitary confinement," and because the negative psychological effects are well documented, the United Nations consider it a torture if it exceeds fifteen days.

We are never alone in our overpopulated world, and when we are, it is rarely by choice, most of the times it is because of some unfortunate events.

Of course, it only lasts ten days, it is not that scary. But you can still see why I had doubts about it.

Finally, the border officers finished the search, and I was cleared to go on my way. I'm someone who loves road trips, and this four-five hours drive from Montreal down to Shelburne, Massachusetts felt like one of those trips. The road was a smooth black river, the sort wheels float so effortlessly along. As my car made its steady way along, the scenery took on an almost meditative quality, the light igniting the hues of each tree and home.

I enjoyed the lovely scenery, listen to some chill music, then let that strange thing that we call stream of consciousness flow uninterrupted.

The roads in this part of the United States are particularly beautiful, there's no much traffic rushing by and you don't feel the usual pression to accelerate, to clear the road. The drivers seem relaxed, they don't have that sad, concentrate expression borderlining depression on their faces that you can see almost everywhere in the big cities.

I would have loved to ride my motorcycle, but I had to much stuff to carry with me than I could stick on it. It would have been a good interlude to my journey though, because riding a bike, as anyone who did it at least once in their life knows, always puts you in a meditative mood.

I reached Shelburne around noon and found my way to the Center. The first impression was as positive as it could be.

Dhamma Dharā Vipassana Meditation Center was a peaceful, delightful place with pristine buildings and well cared surroundings. Surprisingly big, though. That was unexpected. First of all, from a purely mercantile perspective, I was struck by the certainly huge cost of building and maintain such a massive complex. And when you think that all this was possible solely on a donation basis, you have a glimpse into the profound, life-changing effect that the retreat has on people's life.

Many people signed up for this retreat, we were about one hundred souls, women and men. We were greeted by the center volunteers, who assisted us with the formalities.

In one of the forms we were requested to fill in and sign, we were asked a number of questions about our physical and psychological health. We were advised — again — to not attend the retreat if we have some sort of mental issues. This insistence on the mental state arose my curiosity even before I arrived, when I first signed up for the retreat, online. Why would they insist on that detail? Isn't the meditation a form of self-healing? If a person suffers from a mild depression, wouldn't it make more sense that a meditation retreat will help her heal?

Three days later I definitely understood why the insistence. But let's not dive into it at this point.

After we have signed all the forms, we were asked to choose a locker and lock inside all our belongings that had the potential to disturb us during the retreat: phones, computer and tablets, books, magazines, newspapers, agendas, notebooks. We were supposed to enter the premises with nothing but some clothing and bedding items and basic — non-perfumed — toiletries. Because believe it or not, even a pleasant scent could prove to be a source of distractions. I bet nobody thought about the deodorant smell as a distraction before.

They let us know that we can't access our stuff until the end of the retreat, so we should better make the last phone calls right away.

I was so pleased when I found out that I would have my own room! I couldn't imagine how on earth would I be able to abstain from talking and eye contact if I had roommates. It was perfect. A small room with a bathroom, it contained only basic stuff — a bed, a cabinet — but everything was new and clean. Even the view was splendid, from my window I could see the hills, the forest.

Women were separated from men, so that the subtle intersexual dynamic did not affect our concentration. We only met in the grand meditation hall, were women were sited on the right side while men on the left.

We received our schedule: except for the breakfast, lunch and tea break, we basically meditated all day long. We had a five to fifteen minutes pause after every hour of meditation.

Even if meditation wasn't new for me — there's been more than ten years since I begun seriously practicing it — I was never able to rest in a

22

specific posture without moving for more than thirty minutes. My meditation routine includes one or two sessions of maximum 30 minutes per day.

And don't even get me started on the difficulty of trying to keep my racing mind under control for hours!

I didn't check, but I won't be surprised to see that this is also on the UN list of torture methods.

After thirty minutes, lower back and legs start to hurt. After forty to forty-five minutes the perception of time gets greatly altered, every minute seems to last hours long. And this happens when we're not even at the half of the first meditation cycle of the day.

I haven't yet experienced that; all we did the first day was to make ourselves comfortable in our rooms, enjoy a light dinner and participate to a meeting where we were informed about how the retreat will unfold.

We also meet the teachers, male teacher for men, female for women.

The food they served was vegan, and purposely not too abundant. Usually, I don't eat much, but even for me it wasn't merely enough.
We had a breakfast with some basic food like cereals and fruits, a lunch where we were served something slightly more consistent, like rice and beans, and a tea break at around six o'clock, when we had a tea and a fruit. Of course nobody got only one piece of fruit, we were all scared that we would starve to death those twelve hours until the breakfast.

I wondered how I would survive with so little vegan food, I'm not even vegetarian.
But I told myself that if someone like me, who eats relatively small portions of food, is afraid of that, for those who enjoy a little too much eating — and looking around I could see a few who would fall into that category — it will be even harder. If they can make it, so will I.

The first day: doubts are creeping in

The next morning, the first actual day of retreat, the gong rang at 4:30. I wake up dazed from a restless sleep, populated with fragments of meaningless dreams. I proceed to the meditation room. People appear from all directions; I hear doors opening and closing and the stream flows, through the main corridor, towards the great hall. All I see is a sea of feet. When I look up for a moment, I notice that we have all chosen the same strategy to avoid looking at each other: all eyes are on the floor.

It will be the first hour of meditation. I'm excited, impatient. I choose a meditation pillow from the shelves full of benches, chairs, pillows. Unwise choice. I realize pretty soon that my pillow is not at all comfortable. Everything seems fine the first few minutes, then the back pain starts and my legs become numb. I change position but that only moves the pain from one part of the body to another. I don't have a watch — we were asked not to wear watches, and now I understand why — and I don't know how much time is left, but I feel like an eternity has passed.

I'm starting to have doubts: will I be able to resist? It seems improbable. How will I be capable of enduring ten days of ten hours if the first hour is killing me? But then I glance around and I notice that I'm not the only one who suffers.

There is strength in knowing you're not alone. I feel their pain and consequently my own pain becomes bearable.

After the gong announced the end of the first hour of meditation, in the short ten minutes break, I'm rushing to my room and lie down on the floor, trying to relax my back muscles, who are tense as after an intense weight lifting session.

The pain is more severe in the lower back area. I do some basic stretching exercises. I feel that if I don't do this, I won't be able to undergo another hour.

Through what miracle will I be able to endure ten days of ten hours of meditation per day, I wonder? I still don't have a clue about the fact that this isn't going to be the hardest part.

Back to the meditation room. I choose a bench this time, a choice that will prove providential. This way I can slip my feet underneath, avoiding sitting on them. I solved the numbness problem, at least.

I notice some changes in the meditation room. Some of the older colleagues grabbed chairs and moved on the edge of the room, alongside the walls. I sympathize with them. In a moment of weakness, I also have the impulse to choose a chair, then I tell myself that if I decided to keep on, I will make an effort to behave in the same way as most of my colleagues.

The bench indeed solved the numbness problem, but not the back pain. In addition, my buttocks hurt. For the next hour I choose a pillow to cover the bench. This proved to be the final adjustment. I'll keep the same props until the end.

After this second hour of meditation, before breakfast, I stop by my room to do some relaxation exercises.

I then head to the dining room. We are about sixty people, but it's quiet. Everyone takes a plate and serves their preferred meals. Cereals, boiled wheat, jam, margarine, fruit, decaffeinated coffee or tea.

We ate quietly, then some went for a walk through the forest, others returned to their rooms to relax.

I'm in doubt. It took two meditation sessions to realize how much I underestimated the effort and will required to complete this retreat. My back still hurts. In addition, due to the power of habit, I fail to focus on meditation for more than thirty minutes. The rest of the time, my mind is all over the place.

Another hour of meditation and the back pain becomes unbearable. Now it is the pain which prevents me from focusing on meditation. Soon, the pain gets mixed with frustration. How can I focus on meditation under such conditions? And if the pain is going to bother me so much, what's the point of this retreat? It doesn't help telling myself that nothing good comes without suffering. I'm afraid that I'll achieve nothing more than back problems and wasted time. It doesn't seem to be a fair deal. And I was so much looking forward to this retreat!

After another two more hours of meditation, the main meal of the day awaits us. Back in the dining room, back in line with the plates in hand. The food is excellent; we have enough dishes to choose from. Today we equally have dessert.

There are Indian meals and desserts. Simple and tasty.

After we finish eating, we queue for the sink and everyone washes their own plate and silverware. Then we retire to our rooms for an hour of rest.

I'm tired but unable to fall asleep, my thoughts are unsettling. For now, they are strictly related to the situation I'm in, turning around physical pain, but I feel a shadow make its way into my soul and a hint of fear lurks around the edges of my mind.

Waves of enthusiasm are followed by dark thoughts, then vague anxieties.

It is only now that I begin to feel what it means to have nothing to distract your attention. I would like reading something, surfing the internet (How in the hell were our ancestors able to live without internet?!?), I would read and reply to my messages. But I have nothing at hand.

This aspect, the absence of any distractions, will prove vital. The thoughts, over the next few days, will become heavier, more intense, deeper. I will ask myself questions that I have never asked before, I will understand things that I thought I have already understood. I will realize that, despite my conviction that I possess a considerable degree of control over my life, the reality is that most of the time I lived randomly.

I will understand that certain thoughts, experiences, interactions that I thought being normal were completely wrong.

I will understand how I built for myself, without realizing, my own personal brand of hell. This will prove much more painful than the physical pain.

But let's not anticipate.

The meditation day goes on in the afternoon with a couple of one-hour sessions, followed by the evening tea. We are told to choose a fruit, but as we are all starving, we fill our pockets with apples, oranges, bananas. We are aware we won't eat anything else for about twelve hours and this thought makes us uncomfortable.

The last, longest and most difficult session of the day follows. It starts with a recorded video of mister Goenka, the founder of Vipassana centers, played on huge screens. (Daily, at the same hour, the meditation starts with recorded videos being played on screens).

Mr Goenka goes on for a while, talking about what we experienced on this first day and he helps us understand the trials we went through. He laughs at the fact that we filled our pockets with fruits – he taught hundreds of generations of students until his death in 2013; he is obviously familiar with human nature in general and the habits of students in particular. He knew how we would react.

He gives us tips for the next meditation session. He instructs us what to focus on, while explaining why these details are important. We finally understand why we do what we have been told to do.

This session lasts two hours, with a short break between them. After about five minutes of silence, the meditators start changing position, I can feel the restlessness in the room. Almost no one is able to stand still anymore. I make a huge effort to stay put and smoothly adjust my position only when the pain becomes so intense that I can't focus on anything else.

Vanity pushes me to wait until my neighbor moves. It's like a contest; I want to see who gives up first. I am ridiculously trying to prove myself that my pain threshold is higher than anyone else's. The habits of a lifetime follow you everywhere, but usually you don't pay attention to them until you wake up in a context where you can no longer hide from yourself. I didn't realize that I was in this state of mind of permanent competition, that I was living my life as if it was a contest.

I manage to endure until the end. Some colleagues gave up, they retired before the end of the meeting.

We return to our rooms. Half an hour until the lights go out. It's about nine o'clock in the evening. It's totally atypical for me to go to bed so early. I am a night owl, usually I go to bed around three AM and wake up around eleven.

But today I feel exhausted. The first day was a torture from beginning to the end and I did not notice any benefit until the evening session, when I realized that most of the time I was driven by this strange, unconscious, competitive mood. I have thought about this and I can say without any exaggeration whatsoever that this state of mind manifests in almost all areas of my life. I feel like a child who did something wrong and got caught. I feel immature, embarrassed by my immaturity, embarrassed by the fact that I am blind to my own motivation, to my own behavior.

It's time to go to sleep. The final gong of the day just marked the moment. There is absolute silence here, in the middle of nowhere, surrounded by forest, but I can't fall asleep.

Thoughts are racing through my mind; I'm incapable to relax.

Here I am, in an unknown place, surrounded by unknown people, practicing an unfamiliar routine. Nothing around is familiar to me. I miss the things that occupy my free time, books, TV, internet. Here, I don't have the option of tranquilizing myself with the trivial. I miss my friends. I don't know how to enjoy my spare time without all of that.

I realize this was not a new phenomenon; my mind had always darted with the same speed, but I never had the opportunity to set everything aside, for a longer period of time, to make time for introspection.

What awaits me next? This was but the first day.

I finally fall asleep. An even more troubled sleep than the one last night, with intense, vividly coloured dreams, populated by strange characters.

Day two: something is not right

The gong wakes me up again at 4:30. I'm almost happy to hear it, I want to forget this night as soon as possible. I feel exhausted and anxious.

I notice that we are less than yesterday in the meditation room. The desertions have begun.

Methodical concentration on distinct parts of the body seems a blessing now. I can finally focus my mind on something other than my gloomy thoughts.

But then, during the break, the thoughts come back even more vivid, more intense. I'm again wondering what I'm doing here. Not why I chose this retreat, but how I have got here in general, in my life, how a bunch of separate, unconnected decisions affected me, made me take that specific road which brought me here.

How did I get to Canada? Why did I quit my native, familiar Eastern European country, leaving my family and friends behind? I thought I knew why, but all of a sudden I'm not that sure anymore. All my former certitudes look more like rationalizations now; they seem built on sandy foundations.

The reasons I believed made me choose the emigration path are starting to look more like a masquerade. I begin perceiving the true, fundamental motivations, but they are still unclear, wrapped in fog.

I'm starting to understand that I left because I didn't like who I was and how I lived there. I felt the need to start from scratch, to reinvent myself. I like the anonymity of big cities. I like the new beginnings. I wanted to do something with my life, something important that I felt was impossible if I stayed in that place where people have known me since childhood, where they had specific expectations of me, expectations that where in sharp contrast with what I wanted, with the way I understood to live my life.

I realize all this now, still vaguely, for the first time. I left when I was twenty-seven years old and have been living in Canada for fifteen years. I never looked back, I never clarified my reasons for leaving, and I never thought for a second that going back could be an option.

Suddenly I'm not sure about anything anymore.

Twenty-four hours of isolation far from any possible distraction proved enough to realize that my own reasons, the genuine reasons, are almost as foreign to me as those of the noisy neighbor who lives in the apartment above, back home.

What else is waiting for me? I am frightened to anticipate. I entered this retreat center full of certainties and after two days I am already full of doubts.

Every idle moment of the day orients my thoughts with a force impossible to resist, redirecting them again and again toward the essential aspects of my own life.

Meditation sessions, with the related pain, quickly become a good thing, the straw that I'm desperately clinging so as not to drown.

I only found solace in the relaxation exercise of the body, I feel my mind clear and precise, focused on breathing.

The night of the second day is even more dreadful than the first one. My mind is running wildly, in a meaningless zig-zag, between the past, present, and future. It evokes memories I had long forgotten, revive dead feelings, shame, guilt, creates connections between events, sensations, emotions that at first glance did not make any sense.

I feel again like I have absolutely no control over my mind.

Day three: The gates of hell open wide

I hardly slept. I was standing on my bed, legs crossed, back to the wall long before the gong went off. Agitated, I waited for the first meditation hour.

Strange realizations were already beginning creeping out during meditation sessions. I began to feel how tense certain areas of my body were. The abdomen, first of all the abdomen. Eternally tense, as if I were waiting from one moment to another for a punch in the plexus. I lived my whole life without realizing that was tense as a fighter in the ring. It seems that I never knew how it felt to be relaxed.

Not that I managed to totally relax, it seemed obvious to me that there were still parts of the body that I haven't been able to access deep enough.

I wasn't able to concentrate for too long on meditation.

The same kind of thoughts from the day before came back again. But this time, they were more specific and even more painful. I started recollecting emotional experiences from the later part of my life. Fights with friends, lovers. All the rationalizations that I carefully built to justify my actions and my emotional outbursts went crumbling down. Was it really necessary to be so cruel through my words and actions in that last fight with a friend? Yes, he started the fight. Yes, his words wounded me. But was my reaction justified?

I thought so. I thought that it was a perfectly reasonable way to respond to words that hurt me. But now I can clearly see that I overreacted. And the pain that I inflicted to that person came back to haunt me ten times harder. Tears came down my cheeks before I realized what happened with me.

Then I thought about those decisions I made and didn't keep. About how my life would have been different, if I had persevered, in some key areas. I relieved in my mind all those moments when I cruised aimlessly through life, avoiding things I should have done, letting myself down and not giving a damn about it. I had choices and sometimes I chose the easy way out, telling myself that it didn't really matter what I did, I'm only a negligible particle in an inconceivably huge and cold universe.

Nihilism is tempting to fall into. It helps you argue your way out of any action whatsoever, but at what price?

The meditation session finished. We had an hour break.

This was the moment I lost it. All the pain that I could recall inflicting to people in my life came back and hit me hard. I cried as I never did my whole life. I couldn't believe I was so cruel for so long, that I harmed those peoples who loved me. I couldn't believe I didn't realize the fact that by hurting others, I invariably hurt myself. I cried until I had no tears left. Then I cried some more.

It's raining. My room is dark and cold, shadows melting into the darkness.

And I have this moment of supreme clarity, a revelation: I suddenly and clearly understand that we should not do any harm to anyone, that all aggressive, dismissive gestures, hurtful words are coming from what we conceptualize, in the absence of something better, as devil. That doing good deeds or at least ceasing to do the bad tings are the most egotistical actions we can perform, that only by performing those actions we bring peace to our souls.

Those are things that no one can take away from us, that we can always access, even in the most extreme circumstances, like being in prison (they can't remove them from us at the prisons gate), on a hospital bed, at one o'clock in the morning, the terrible hour of extreme lucidity or even in a

43

mundane setting like this quiet, dark, cold room with huge rain drops hitting the window.

I understand that nothing is as bitter and closer to hell than the memories of ugly, evil, petty deeds; than the emptiness of unused talents, wasted gifts; that, therefore, it is proper to do good while there is still time, before reaching the state in where we can't do it anymore.

I understand that by gathering beautiful memories (but not the regret of a few moments of fleeting pleasure, because this is also torment), we build our own paradise, which is only a sum of good deeds, noble or heroic actions, or generous behavior.

Put differently, God is completely absent from the world, but he is also entirely present within us. God is eminently present to the soul and even immediately recognizable. We only need accessing our inner self. If we are capable of accomplishing this, we will always know how to live, how to behave in any particular circumstances.

You don't need a religion or sacred text to comprehend that. You merely need accessing that part of your soul that can't be reached while living your day to day life.

You need to walk away from all distractions to be able to have a genuine conversation with yourself.

All religions insist on loving your neighbor like you love yourself. The Bible goes even further and asks you to turn the other cheek, when slapped. We struggle to understand this, and no wonder: it doesn't make a lot of sense, rationally speaking. But now I understand that we generally have a wrong way of conceptualizing this. We don't do them a favor by loving them, neither by turning the other cheek, but we do ourselves a huge favor. We build our own heaven by doing something meaningful for the others, even for those we can easily argue they do not deserve it. In essence, what we do is on some level an egotistical action, which is fundamentally good for all those concerned and for the society, the world altogether. It is a genuinely win-win situation.

I would be amazed by our ancestors' insight if I weren't aware they lived a more meaningful and more uncomplicated life than us, which means they were more in tune with their own conscience.

I'm aware that the turning the other cheek could nevertheless be seen as a rather extreme gesture, but hear me out on this: what you lose by doing this is insignificant — in most cases — when you're looking at the big picture.

You could lose on short term but if you put in balance the gain for your own soul, there's no doubt left about which is more important.

The implication of this understanding is even more profound: I asked myself why the memories of wrongdoings are so painful and the memories of good deeds so heart-warming? Could it be because of the culture we live in? Could the culture shape us so efficiently that we suffer if we breach the spoken or even unspoken rules? It could be but I doubt it, and here's why: I felt pain even for some things that culturally speaking are acceptable. It means my feelings resurfaced from a more deeper, more ancient level.

You can build a case that all I say is irrelevant: I could have been influenced by some personal psychological imbalances, but this hypothesis won't explain why most of the people I spoke to at the end of the retreat had similar experiences. And it will be an overreach to suggest everybody had some sort of shared mental issue.

So, why are the memories of wrongdoings so painful? The bad things that happened to us don't seem to really count; it seems like the others don't have power over us in the long run. Why is it inevitable to hurt ourselves when we hurt someone else? The only reasonable conclusion seems to be that we are all coming from the same place. We are all one, as the

Buddhists so often says (say). We are all manifestations of the same divine principle.

I can't go further than that. My limited self can't grasp what this divine principle is and through which processes we ended up embodying it.

But there's no need to go further, to try to understand the non-understandable. I now have all the tools I need to live a meaningful life. I could do more and longer retreats to gain an even deeper insight, but it won't alter the ultimate truth: that most of the time we are the ones responsible of creating our own heaven and hell.

Day 4 - 6 back on my feet again. More soul searching (with a material side dish)

The fourth day I wake up, after another agitated night, with the same psychological pain. I can't stop reliving my life and judging it in the light of this new mindset I just acquired. The yesterday's agony is back. I struggle against a strong impulse to just leave and go ask for forgiveness from all the people I ever hurt.

I understand now why they insisted so much on discouraging those with psychological issues to attend. I can imagine how a person prone to, let's say, panic attacks, would react to something so overwhelming. Or someone who is already depressed. It could turn fast ugly.

The gong calls us to the first meditation of the day. While walking toward the meditation room, I can hear someone sobbing in his room. I'm surprised, then relieved. It means that I'm not the only one going through this pain.

We are visibly fewer in the meditation hall. The third day was a stepping stone for most of us, it seems.

I try to concentrate on different body segments, as the meditation hour unfolds. To my surprise it works pretty well. I still experience emotional pain, but I'm starting to feel a slight, unexpected relief. It's the beginning of the healing process.

We went for the breakfast. I'm curious to see my colleagues, to guess their struggle from their expression. And I have no more doubt about it: almost everybody seems gloomy. It is surprising how little time of isolation we need to get back in sync with our fundamental human nature.

I still can't hold my tears for the rest of the day, but the anguish feeling starts to slowly fade out. I'm beginning assuming all the mistakes I made, telling myself I didn't know what I was doing and promising myself to never let that happen again. Now I know. There's no excuse anymore.

I'm able to concentrate more on the meditation. During the next few days, my focus is getting steadily better. I feel less pain while sitting in meditation posture for hours. I can go deeper in my body now; the relaxation is more profound.

I'm just sitting there, and I'm feeling happy. I don't need anything else; everything is perfect as it is. I'm breathing deeply and slowly, amazed at how good it feels. I'm grateful that I'm healthy, that my spirit is not agitated anymore. I'm grateful that the people I love, family, friends, past and actual lovers are still around and healthy, that I live in a beautiful country in peace time, that I have the freedom to choose my own path in life, to carve my own destiny.

I realize my life is way better than I ever thought it would be, despite all the wrong choices I made or good ones I failed to make.

Outside of meditation, my mind, once it freed itself from the grip of torment, starts to reevaluate life from a different perspective, a more practical one. I can clearly see now that the life I lived was as random and reckless as my spiritual life, that I was lost, I was drifting aimlessness, that I didn't really have a plan. I was just waiting for whatever opportunity comes my way, and hoping that the outcome will be ok.

It seems obvious that if you don't know what you want, then it doesn't really matter where you go, or what you do. You will be pulled in different directions by random events, by other people who have dreams, goals, and plans.

And this is exactly what happened. My job is not the one I dreamed of, it hardly could be, as I never really thought seriously what I wanted to do in life. I didn't choose some of the people I called friends, they just stumbled upon me and I accepted them in my world without questions.

One of the things I voluntarily chose to do was travelling. I don't regret travelling; I did it for about 10-12 years and enjoyed every second of it, the only problem is that while I was always focused on the next destination, I didn't really care about my personal or professional life. I didn't budget, I had debt accumulating, I didn't own a house and I never thought about retirement.

It seems paradoxical to think about debt, owning a house or retirement while on a spiritual quest. If someone had told me this me this before, I would have probably laughed it off. But now I realize the importance of sorting out those multiple layers of our life, in order to be able to enjoy as much as possible our time on earth.

It is hard to be equanimous when debt is accumulating and your family is suffering.

I don't say that it is impossible to enjoy a rich spiritual life if your practical, material situation is unideal, what I'm saying is that it is harder. And you want to put all chances on your side.

I don't need much food anymore and my body got used to fasting for 12 hours on a daily basis. I stopped stuffing my pockets with fruits at dinner time. Most of the guys stopped. We realized we probably wouldn't starve to death, even if all our life experience suggested this outcome. We were wrong. How surprising.

Do you remember those commercials for Snickers when the guy who was hungry looked like a beast before eating a candy bar? I'm sure it is a familiar feeling for most of us. We get irritated when hungry. But guess what: if you are able to keep yourself in check for 3-5 days, you will bypass that physical reaction. You won't feel it anymore, it will be gone for good. Our bodies are amazing machines.

I'm starting enjoying my surroundings in new, profound ways. I always loved being outdoor, walking, hiking. But I never felt the impulse, like I feel right now, to stop during my daily walks and touch the trees. I pick up leaves and examine them: they are slightly withered but still smooth, thin, fragile. I'm looking at all this complexity and marvel: how come all of this was possible? And why don't we devote any attention whatsoever to them? Miracles are happening all over around us, but we don't see them.

I contemplate the wind playing with fallen leaves, and conceive my old self like one of them, a blown leaf turning around through the air, who wavers and tumbles to the ground.

I walk in the forest deliberately, feeling the earth underneath my feet, soft, pleasant, while breathing consciously the sweet perfumed forest fragrance.

From time to time I stumble upon small forest animals and birds. We observe each other; I contemplate them with an amalgam of curiosity and wonder, and they observe me with a mixture of nervousness and inquisitiveness.

Day 7 - 9. The healing process

The intense emotional feelings subside as days go by. I am able to concentrate more and more on the actual act of meditation.

The thought of an uninterrupted hour, sitting without moving, doesn't frighten me at all anymore. I enjoy it now. It is with the pauses between meditations that I don't know how to deal.

Starting with the 7th day, each of us are assigned a cell in the Pagoda. They are small, closet-like rooms, three feet long, three large, completely dark, with a good sound isolation.

I love my cell. I can't wait to go there to meditate in absolute isolation. It felt so good that at one point I started actually contemplating a monastic life. Maybe I have a monastic vocation, if the isolation makes me feel so good, I thought to myself. I'm not talking about the overexcited type of happiness, like the one when you win the lottery, but a steady, equal flow of warm, good feelings.

I can imagine now the monks happy. Until recently I had this misconception that they must be lonesome and miserable with brief moments of bliss.

I'm quarantined at home while I put together this book, we are in the middle of the pandemic outbreak and I'm so glad that I had the chance of experiencing the silent retreat before this period. Now I can thoroughly enjoy the isolation, while some of my fellow citizens succumb to dread, the depression rates are getting higher than ever, people snap at each other for irrelevant reasons, they are gloomy and demoralized.

I would likely feel the same, but I know better now. I remember I thought at one point during my retreat that even if I were sentenced to prison following a judicial error, let's say, locked in an isolation chamber, I would find it a perfect opportunity to deepen my meditation skills, because I know nothing else brings me more of a steady, quasi-permanent joy that this; and I don't need anything to do it. I'll always have with me all I need — my body — and nobody can't take it away.

And it makes sense, as paradoxically as it sounds, if you think about it: you have a shelter, and someone else is taking care of your food. You don't need to think about anything; you're able to intently concentrate on your meditation practice.

I realize how strange it sounds; I'm also aware you can't fully understand a seemingly outrageous statement like this if you didn't experience the inward joy that you are able to unlock by using meditation techniques. Culturally speaking, we are uninclined to live an inward focused live. We are accustomed to keep ourselves busy, to overindulge on distractions, to keep away the uncomfortable feeling of emptiness. We are not masters of our domains. When someone or something take those distractions away from us, we can't fill the vacuum; we never even tried to develop that skill.

While meditating in my Pagoda cell, I had some moments that I could describe as a sneak-peek into illumination, as I conceptualize it. For a couple of seconds, I got overwhelmed by this intense feeling of bliss, by an almost unbearable happiness. I felt like being immersed in an ocean of light, floating on the top of the world, feeling nothing else than intense joyfulness. It never lasted more than 30-40 seconds, but I was thankful that I had the chance to understand what life could be if I devoted myself to a spiritual path.

Those moments were few and far between, but there was something else that always stayed with me: a feeling of calmness, of peace. I felt joyful in a stable, consistent way. My meditation cell in Pagoda is the ultimate isolation and it felt so good that every time I had to make an effort to get up and walk out.

It is strange how fast I switched from psychological distress to this blissful state I found myself within during the last 2-3 days of my retreat. I suppose that's life, when you make a radical change, things will often get worse before turning better.

I felt sorry for the people that gave up after the first two, three days. They merely experienced the agony. They didn't have the chance to see what's on the other side of the suffering. They most likely missed one of the most meaningful experience of their life.

In only two days of meditation cell, I developed a "super-power": I became able to raise the temperature of my body. More than that, I became able to raise the temperature of a specific body part, like, let's say, my left arm or my right leg. It must have something to do with the fact that, while concentrating intensely on a specific body part, the blood flow increases in that area. I have had a bad blood flow in my feet since childhood, so it was pleasant to be able to warm them using nothing but the power of mind.

I thoroughly enjoyed my last days of retreat. I still felt physical pain now and then; I still felt guilt while reflecting on my past, but the main mindset was an overwhelming desire to start my life over again, and do it better.

I felt the urge to reset myself, to allow everything that it's not worth preserving die and develop what now I know is essential. I was full of hope.

The last day: The Big Reset

The gong woke us up, for the last time. We went to the meditation hall. It was the last group meditation, after which we were free to look at each other, to speak to each other.

My entire meditation consisted in visualizing my new life, my new goals. I was excited like a child about all the possibilities that awaited me out there.

"I will so much miss the meditation hall, my Pagoda cell, my minimalist room," I thought. But maybe I will be able to adapt my apartment so it looks more like this rather than how it looks now, a sort of gadget exposition.

My colleagues were noisier, they shifted position often, everybody seemed overly excited. I'm pretty sure most of them had new life projects and they couldn't wait to make them happen.

We went to the lunchroom, for the breakfast. We passed through the clean, long hall with rooms on both sides. Doors opened and closed, people entered and exited, we looked at each other and smiled. We were officially not allowed to speak until breakfast time and everybody seemed to follow the rule. We learned that every rule we were asked to follow during the retreat proved beneficial to us in a way or another, so we didn't feel the need to rebel against them anymore.

As I was approaching the lunchroom, I begun to hear the chatter. Voices grew stronger as I got closer.
I reached the room, opened the door and closed it back right away. It was louder than I could handle. Too much noise and I weren't used to it anymore. I lingered in the hall for some time, greeting and being greeted by those passing by.
We were not segregated anymore, men and women walked by me talking to each other, cups of coffee in hands.

I finally mustered the courage to enter the crowded, rowdy room.

It was strange to hear my own voice after ten days of silence. It seemed unfamiliar. The things I said seemed irrelevant. I kind of asked myself: "Why bother to speak if you don't say anything substantial?" But I knew the answer: it is a form of bonding, of sharing, of familiarizing yourself with the other.

I also realized how strangely fulfilling is to talk less and listen more.

I had a conversation with some of my colleagues. We shared our experience. I wasn't surprised to learn the third day was the most difficult for nearly all of them. One of the guys, a middle aged man from New Jersey, told me that he felt an incredible urge to run away, literally run and never look back. Another one, a tall, fit guy in his 50's, said that he thought he would go crazy that day, but then he saw his room mate quietly crying in his corner and a strong feeling of empathy flooded his heart. He felt it would be cruel to leave him alone, suffering.

Some younger people didn't seem to have experienced the same things as most of us. One of them told us proudly that he managed to keep his phone, and he talked every night with his friends. He didn't realize the importance of getting rid of all distractions. I wasn't aware either, initially, but now I knew what a game changer this proved to be.

I was curious to talk to a woman also, but the one I spoke to, a young Filipino girl, proved to be a veteran of these retreats: it was her fifth one. She enjoyed every moment of it, but she didn't feel particularly overwhelmed, like most of us. For her it became a way of life, every year she comes back to do it again, it keeps her on the right path, as she explains. I examined her attentively: there was a steadiness to her, as if all the storms in the world were no more than a whispering breeze, once they reach her. "I'm not there yet," I muttered to myself. But I know the road, I have the map.

I left Dhamma Dhara at around one o'clock in the afternoon. I drive slowly, enjoying the ride through the forest area.
I rolled the windows down and each breath of the fresh, pine scented air filled me with a sense of joy that almost made me want to shout out loud, just to hear my voice echo amidst the trees.

I left the retreat with a soul so vibrant that it began to merge with every living thing, radiating, resonating; I was fortunate enough to catch a glimpse at a modest, fulfilling, grateful way of life that is the only kind worth living. I felt closer than ever to paradise. The only possible paradise: the one designed and built by oneself.
Or maybe I died and was reborn.

Aftermath (a year later)

I deliberately waited a year before publishing this memoir. Why?

Because I knew that life happens. That I will go back to the rat race, responsibilities, things to fix, dishes to wash, bills to pay. And I knew that some of the things I so vividly lived would fade out.

I wanted to give you an idea about what happens in the real world with the insight that one gains during the silent meditation retreat.

I tried sticking to a meditation routine of two hours a day, one in the morning, one in the afternoon. That didn't work out: in the afternoon, after work, I was so tired and energetically depleted that I wasn't able to meditate.

About two months later, the one-hour morning meditation begun to get shorter, especially towards the end of the week. I realized I didn't like meditating in a sitting position, so I started doing it lying down, on my back. This trick — albeit for a Vipassana practitioner a sacrilege — proved to be a game changer; it saved my practice. I loved it. I did it during the day, for short periods of times. About six months in, I got back to about one hour a day.

So the thing that got me back on track was a posture adaptation.

One thing never changed: the revelation I experienced, about how I built my own hell, lingered in my soul. It is still as vivid as it was back then. This is something I'm certain I will never forget.

This idea had a profound impact on me. It reoriented my life. I'm way more aware about my shortcomings during social interactions. I'm more patient, more understanding.

It doesn't always work, unfortunately. Every so often I react before thinking it through, other times I know what I'm doing is wrong, but I'm doing it anyway. It will be a lifelong quest, I suppose. It is hard to rewire your brain after years of bad habits.

I can undoubtedly see progress. Those things happen less and less as the time passes by.

I see now in a new light religious books or books about religious experiences, like the last years' journal of Leo Tolstoy. I remember   first time I tried to read it: I gave up after several pages; I didn't understand a thing, it seemed to me the mumbling of an old man, too close to death and afraid of it. Now I realize the profound insight of this remarkable writer and understand the undeniable fact that we can all achieve the same conclusions, following different paths.

I wish I could be articulate enough to be able to persuade everyone about the importance of not engaging in hurtful, dismissive gestures and words; to make them understand that if they do, it will definitely come back to haunt them.

To help them realize how terribly painful is your personal kind of hell and how easy and rewarding is to build your heaven instead.

But I can't seem to pass the message convincingly enough. People listen politely sometimes, but usually they don't take it seriously. And I don't blame them. Nothing beats personal experience when it comes to learning.

That's why I think that for a person who's on a spiritual journey, Vipassana silent meditation retreat represents an accelerated learning curve.

It is probably one of the most meaningful experience one could live.

It definitely was, for me.

Adrian Benea grew up in Brasov, Romania. He graduated from Transylvania University with a Bachelor's degree in Sociology, and later from Concordia University with a Web Development degree. He is a registered yoga teacher who teaches Yoga Nidra and meditation classes in Montreal, Canada.

Printed in Great Britain
by Amazon